OLD WOMAN OF IRISH BLOOD

"Irish nature is characterized by a passionate
yearning towards the vague, the mystic, the
invisible, and the boundless infinite of the realms
of imagination....The Irish love youth, beauty,
splendour, lavish generosity, music, and song,
the feast and the dance....The deep pathos
of Irish nature finds its fullest representation
in the tender, plaintive, spiritual music of the
wail and lamentations of the Banshee [a spirit
in female form who wails as death nears.]"

Lady Wilde, *Ancient Legends of Ireland*, 1988

OLD WOMAN
of Irish Blood

Pat Andrus

For Alexie,
Great maker of words,
of the sacred language.
On poetry and peace.

Pat Andrus
9/21/97

OPEN HAND PUBLISHING INC.
Seattle, Washington

OPEN HAND PUBLISHING INC.
P. O. Box 22048
Seattle, WA 98122-0048

Cover painting:
Tired Lady, 1969, by William Dobell (1899-1970)
Oil on canvas on hardboard, 121.5 x 121.5 cm
The Art Gallery of New South Wales

Design and production: Deb Figen
Art & Design Services, Seattle, Washington

Library of Congress Cataloging-in-Publication Data

Andrus, Pat. 1943 -
    Old Woman of Irish Blood / Pat Andrus.
        p. cm.
    ISBN 0940880-59-8
    1. Irish American women--Poetry. 2. Irish Americans--Poetry.
I. Title.
PS3551.N4567043 1996
811'.54--dc20   95-42423
                                                            CIP

FIRST EDITION • FIRST PRINTING
Printed in the United States of America

99 98 97 96 • 6 5 4 3 2 1

NATIONAL
ENDOWMENT
FOR THE
ARTS

This project is supported by a grant from
the National Endowment for the Arts

Dedicated to
Larry and Kira

•

In memory of
Maurine E. Andrus

Contents

Foreword

As you squat over the fire
steaming potatoes and singing runes
I remember
I touch the earth around you
feel it moan in response

Old Woman

In *Old Woman of Irish Blood*, poet Pat Andrus
explores the mysterious roots of her artistry, her
own tree of power; the way in which her Celtic sap
rises, pumping through the delicate soft veins of
every facet of life, daily or lyrical (or daily and
lyrical); the way that her self, through the self of her
blood, is inseparable from what we call Nature,
human or not. Everywhere in this collection
appears the tree, the sea, the feather, the bone:
icons of transcendent natural beauty. The poet lives
"to touch bee fuzz, smell horse sweat, / hear
whippoorwill music." These poems bespeak this
poet's palpably sensual communion with the
natural world, often expressed in the metaphor of
Druidic, mytho-poeic forces. Fate-like female elders
("leather-skinned goddesses") dream nursery
rhymes as the speaker of the poem, in her quest to
bring forth the runes of her lifetime story, listens
"for a sign from crow's screeches," willing to have
"rolled in pine needles and birch leaves / thirsty for
secrets my bones told me."

Sometimes, reading a Pat Andrus poem from this collection is like climbing a tree of power — at other times, it is like falling into a well of powers, where silence moves to a different rhythm and darkness crawls your skin. The inward movement of her personal and cultural self-scrutiny is that concentrated, that intensely focused, because the poet knows how even the homely runes carved on her "bathroom mirror / can reveal tales." The mirror appears again and again in this collection, a witness to the fact that Andrus finds her own artistic truths encoded not only in earth, tree, and sky, but also in family history. The presence of the mother and the daughter as subjects of more than one song in this collection reminds us of the spiritual trinity of gender suggested by the title of the work: grand mother, mother, daughter — each destined, should she live, to be the "old woman," the spiritual seer for the following generations.

The idea of generation leads us to a delicate irony: that the British colonization of, among others, Irish and African peoples, should one day produce an American poet who defends the oppressed (the murdered prostitutes, degraded wives, and harried welfare mothers in "Carrie Rois"). The narrow supremacy of the few, then, can be challenged by the diversity of all creation. In this age of emerging multiculturalism, four years from the twenty-first century, *Old Woman of Irish Blood* speaks to us in multifarious tongues. It tells us from where this artist's art comes: the cultures of Ireland

and America, the culture of gender, the culture of
love ("this house of pain"), the culture of art even as
it adores nature — or explores ethnic origins. Ethnic
self-awareness guides Pat Andrus as she follows the
Celtic heart beating below her European-American
face.

Finally, the diversity of these realities lives as
an integrated plurality in the body of these poems:

> Then come back another way
> be an eagle soaring
> be a salmon swimming home to your river
> be your daughter crying for your return.

Donna J. Meek
Seattle, Washington

Acknowledgments

Some of the poems in **Old Woman of Irish Blood** appear in the following publications: *Arnazella, Backbone, Bellowing Ark, Blue Unicorn, Colorwheel, Crosscurrents, Hawaii Review, Perspectives, Sage Woman, Spindrift, Wildflower,* and *Z Miscellaneous.*

"Daughters of Artemis" was originally published in the author's letterpress collection *Daughter,* Olivewood Press, 1987.

"The Gold-Taloned Mirrors" appears in the anthology *Motherhood: A Feminist Perspective,* Haworth Press, 1990.

"Kira's Tanka" was published in the Mirrors International Tanka Award Collection *Tanka Splendor,* AHA Books, 1992.

"A Poet's Round," "Erin's Story," "I'm in a Stuck Zone," "The Demoiselle Remembered," "This Holy," "Genesis," and "This Winter Rain" are recorded on the tape *Beágan: The New Branch* by Charles Dews, Pat Andrus, and musician and singer Mariana Van Blair, Toora Loora Loora Press / Spoken Arts, 1991.

Well of Powers

Split one day from a tender ledge,
I rolled like granite into an empty well.
Darkness immediately crawled my skin.
The ground, almost warm, held
rotting leaves, gum wrappers, rusty coins,
fodder for this marooned poet.

I could have screamed my name,
making tiny tunnels for climbing out,
the air so unused to human cries.
I could have made songs using
this thick time, compose a book
of sonnets, write an elegy
for my most certain death.

But silence held in a well
moves to different rhythms. It now
pushes the mind awake, and presses flesh
against well's side, soon
finding braces circling
this hole. And sun,
playing at well's entrance,
charges muscles alive.

So I crawled out, boosted by
my determination again
to touch bee fuzz, smell horse sweat,
hear whippoorwill music.

These days I tell children
to paint their faces like a bird
or animal.

"You'll grow powers for climbing out of wells."

This sputtering makes them giggle.
Yet they draw all the same, tasting
their creature's skin
as their own faces turn
first toward each other,
then out to the sun.

First Delivery

My uterine muscles
push you out of
your 19 week old home
through a birth canal
unprepared for your body
tiny and now dying
after nine hours of labor

and blood
and the little water left
and my next contraction
carry you into blinding light
and cold hospital sheets
where two attending nurses
whisk away the several parts of
your dead birth

and this,

after the water has broken
your sustenance for survival
gushing down my legs
lost between bathroom cracks

after the two month bed rest
when I thought we had made it
that my womb had protected
your growing

after my hemorrhaging in the theater
where my husband
drove us home in silence
and failure formed a cloud
we both appended to my title
as Mother

But here, now,
in this hospital room,
I think you must be deformed
I feel, with all those pieces
splattering onto the mattress,
that this miscarriage
is meant to be,
that really, you couldn't
even have been whole yet

and not yet three weeks later
the doctor makes his report:
A boy, perfect specimen.
He continues, as if
giving me a soothing tonic:
One in three pregnancies
end in a natural abortion
Don't get upset
No big deal
We'll try again

yet here, also,
in my hospital bed
you, my lost one,
you, who breaks my heart,
who takes parts of me away
in your dying,
will also gift me with fire
and like the phoenix
I will rise before the doctor's face
burn his words
in my own dance of grief and rage
bring to life my own new self

and another
I will deliver 18 months later
with a healer I find
through the strength
you leave me
my lovely miscarried one

Old Woman

I sometimes see you
old woman
maybe a hag
if I look at you straight
I find you gathering roots by the river
muttering their names like psalms
yellow dock   valerian   sanicle

your body covered with layers of wool
stuck together by sweat and grease

Today I want to get close to you
listen for those smacking gums
As you squat over the fire
steaming potatoes and singing runes
I remember
I touch the earth around you
feel it moan in response

Ancient one
you sit through the night
watch with the moon
finger the dirt
you hold me still
your potion of silence

How do I offer you anything?
sit on the damp ground
dig my nails into my face
hope for blood or a scar
your gifts?

Old woman
I want to see your home
find out where you call your dead sisters
sign those songs you moan
but they say you leave tomorrow
taking away your roots
your secrets

Then come back another way
be an eagle soaring
be a salmon swimming home to your river
be your daughter crying for your return

Ward 5-B

The menus are individualized
and I'm caught between apple pie and chocolate cake
but the door swings open to shiny chrome
and the cart with the electrified box moves in
I need to leave for only twenty minutes
my roommate is being juiced
to forget it all
to get herself ready to walk out
ten visits in fifteen days
not bad for one stay

This isn't my home
and my burning chest won't help
I wander the halls to help others
find some time to watch tv.
but shouldn't I become a candidate
have my memories burned
get my smile prepared for the open door

These nurses take my life by shifts
hold me mornings when I scream for my breath
close my eyes at night with thorazine
but they don't walk my dreams with me
and a box of wires can't reach that deep

In the next room I find this fat woman
she or she/he has been watching me
we play cards or drink beer in the Terry Bar
but she has a nasty past
people still roll her for coins
her lover beats her by day
and even welfare will get her axed
fourteen days and she's out

cured according to the laws of the state
and this big woman in baggy pants
asks ME about her health
ME! Who takes Menu #48 with cake

The padded room is arranged by squares
square walls
square ceiling
square pads
square pillows
I rip two a week
feathers fly when I pound them
the nurses smile
they will give me a star

They call it occupational therapy
to occupy time after lunch
we make beaded necklaces
thirty beads on each safety pin
fifty safety pins for each necklace
fifteen hundred beads
this is occupational therapy
I can make necklaces but
I can't see beyond these beads
this project would send me mad outside

So I look at my roommate's friend
She calls lovers friends
she calls acquaintances friends
she, my roommate's friend,
is attractive in my roommate's clothes
they trade outfits and cry when her friend leaves
they make love when I sleep or when I walk
down the ward

And the days go around like a ferris wheel
and our fathers and mothers are far away
going over their own tales of denial
saying a litany each day for the sick
while I carve out the next day's meat
holding my knife to the veal cutlet
that appears on Menu #48

Genesis

for Michael Patrick and Ryan James

There is no reason
for us to shake
in the sea of our beginnings
for our fragile bones, lifted out
of womb, come with water and skin,
and a heart
determined to live one more life

and our tender lungs, raw from air
we choke on these first moments,
push us to speak to this world, if only
through a squeak, or a wail, or if lucky
one long cry of intention

and our blood, salty and fertile
equips us for this next journey
gifts us like that original sea
the pool of collective openings, closings
where bones from all the world
form and crumble

So do not fear the sea of our beginnings
it holds the runes of each lifetime story,
and its bold waves are only
shaping and reshaping
the shores we crawl to and from

One Sentence Dedicated to Carrie Rois

Carrie Rois, one of the Green River murderer's 48 victims

There are no juries and no witnesses and the ten million
dollar funded Green River Task Force spews out green and
white personalized jackets, and the bodies continue their
surfacing and a name like Carrie floats through the
headlines like discolored print and there is no big funeral
with food and drink afterwards, and the minister saying
she was a good young woman doesn't get said

and there is nothing to say to you, Carrie, because most of
us really don't know how old you were and if you had a
brother or sister or if you lived on the streets or if you had
children, and yet there is one thing we all know and that
is the fact that you were woman of woman born

and then the I, that is the I of being woman must step in
here because I know Carrie was as surely murdered as I
know women are not protected in this country and
women are not taught to protect each other and, in fact,
women are urged to be separate from one another and to
think that a prostitute, for example, is more degraded than
a wife, a wife meaning the decorated ornament in the
moneyed home of a man, a woman who participates in
her husband's wealth, got from places where at some
point down the line people are treated like slaves because
they are paid a wage that no one can live on or, a wife,
meaning a wife from a family that doesn't have enough
money and who goes out to earn that 60 cents on a dollar
and who is blamed for going to work because her children
will then have to languish in daycare, and

the daycare is not protected by good government
regulations because the government, paid by us, does not
value children in any real way whatsoever, and if she, this

mother, this wife, stays home, the children do not get
attention by any other caring adults, but stay with the
same caretaker and that caretaker, this mother, does not
get paid anything for taking care of our future generation,
and this mother will not get any social security for her
labor when she retires because the government does not
recognize her work as a caretaker of children, and if she
stays home, the children starve

and so, if Carrie had been a mother, she might have gone
out to do tricks so that her children would not starve
because if she had worked at McDonald's she would have
starved, along with her children, and this hamburger
place doesn't pay medical benefits, although they are
all for America and care for all of us if you see their
commercials, but they do not care for all of their
employees, really, and their wages do not even pay for
food if you need to pay the rent, so Carrie's kids could
have gotten food as long as they didn't mind sleeping
under viaducts and getting sick from exposure

but maybe Carrie didn't have kids or maybe she was quite
young and was told by television and the ads in Mademoiselle that she had to have pretty clothes and a good
figure and be someone, and I mean really someone cool,
and that the boys in her neighborhood were the only
authorities, when it came right down to it, who could
really tell her what she was worth

and if Carrie had been black, or brown, or some color
other than the flour white paste in Mademoiselle or in the
commercials on television, she figures she would get a
better break, maybe, on the streets, instead of going to
some place to work where they pay less money to women
who are black, or brown, or red or who have eyes that are

a slightly different shape than those women in Mademoiselle, and though the work place would not pay less right
away, necessarily, it would begin to pay less if the women
did not want to do the right things, like take classes in the
evening to get slim, or play the same power games and eat
the same food and have their language be exactly right, I
mean exactly male white

and maybe some of this occurred to Carrie, who at some
level probably could not stomach that particular life, which
is really nothing different because the work the women do
if they got up near the top, would still be just a play in that
game, and the women would become less than ever of what
they thought they were and, anyway, the women would
probably have to have initials after their names, like M.B.S.,
from a diploma mill, and probably even then, they would
still at some point have to obtain the Mademoiselle look

so Carrie, maybe, was going to get tricks, which at least
seemed a little more straight, and of course Carrie would
not have known right away about pimps, but then there are
pimps, and then there are what is known as husbands, and
did she know the difference in the *legal* sense, and *is* there a
difference in the legal sense, since in most states a man can
rape his wife and it is not called rape and it is not illegal

and maybe Carrie, at some point, liked to take a little hit
here and there, but then again how is that different from
the housewife who works the 60 cents on the dollar having
a beer, or the ornamental wife snorting some coke, and
what is the difference

and why don't we all know more about Carrie, since we too
could look in the mirror any morning and be murdered that
same night?

For Clara on Her First Christmas

Clara,
your teddy bear watches over you
as you shake and squirm
in your struggle to crawl toward her,
and the holly branches
placed on the oak table
send runic messages
your new cells hear.

And Clara,
it seems the world pauses
when you reach for bulbs on the Yule pine
as if the health of our entire planet
depends on how a six-month-old sprig
reacts to ornaments on one tree;
as if we dare to hope for peace
if only you squeal when your Siamese, Max,
sniffs your nose before escaping;
or if you smile when one of us
is captured by that Gemini gaze.

And so, Clara,
we continue our vigil,
wait for your first word,
chart your weight when you gain
another pound, count the times
you gurgle in your sleep.

But elders gather the most important facts:
how you dream gardens of pink chrysanthemums
the sky flooded with butterflies;
that you and teddy fly to distant planets,
the glow of Mars lighting your way.

Tasting Clover and August Sun

First it was the geraniums
rough textured leaves, crisp
raw smell, the blossoms'
fire red clumps

then the roses
that told me tender would never
float into my descriptions
except for rose petals their
silkened lips

and later on tomato plants
branches whose scent grew out of
manure, or rotting grass, or mix
of dirt and heat
and their fruit made me question
my sterile days, so sweet
and succulent their meat and juice

six summers ago
I see orange pink rock, boulders
with pieces decorating feet
of wild sage
I nearly get rear-ended when
I spot these stones, slamming on
my breaks before pulling into
a canyon's mouth
believing and not believing
this granite of salmon tones

but before all this
my daughter's breath
two minutes after birth
her face near mine
such fragrant perfume
I try telling the doctor
bottle this
and how do I keep her breath
that makes heaven for me?
Then I pass out from birth pains
and nurses bottle feed her, say
my milk was too late in coming,
my heaven disappearing

this morning one Morgan foal
racing through a country pasture
I coax it to eat grass from my hand
and its tongue rich with clover
and August sun
convinces me to head
for my local prison
in one more effort to persuade
the warden, this time, to let prisoners
go to that pasture
gallop over that land
so they can taste the clover
and the sun

The Gold-Taloned Mirrors

This child, my daughter.
We go blind from mirrors
jagged pieces we both wear
and mirrors cut my cave
and my daughter child cries
raw reflections scarring her face

but if she sings
I drop
hungry for love
and my lost dreams
crawl toward dawn
falling into these mirrors at sunrise
now decorated with gold talons
holding pictures of
sheaves of wheat

and a crystal ball
hangs from one frame
telling me it's here
it's all here
this light
this house of pain
I call love

Female Elders Dream Nursery Rhymes

painted in purple and blood tones
spread out to ancient horizons
and their bodies, acting like huge alembics,
work feverishly through the night
to obtain the pure gold
the symbols these dreamers
gather for their final homecoming
In daylight they soak in palm oil
wash their hair with okra juice
call us from our own dance
to keep watch
when they sing in mumbled verse

but listen, my leather-skinned goddesses
if your teeth chatter while speaking
your arms crossed in frozen poses
if your eyes send empty messages
then I must delay attending your vigil

for I've waited each year
four times, in four seasons
to walk in country gardens
sniff for scent of ripening seeds
listen for a sign from crow's screeches
I've followed trails where fog settles
away from pink-shadowed sun paths
felt grey cold encircling my lungs
as I've looked for wild bushes
thick with moisture
And I've sprinkled the spores
of a boletus on my stomach

rolled in pine needles and birch leaves
thirsty for secrets my bones told me
I might find here

yet if any of you
were to uncross your arms
stare at me with a rattlesnake's gaze
maybe as I felt your power in my body
if I started to change into owl feathers
float toward a salt beach or the forest floors
then my own dreams might create colors
take me to images I left long ago
and I would beg to help in the okra wash
begin songs with words
from your mumbled verse

But until then only runes
carved in cracks on my bathroom mirror
can reveal tales I might believe
and my own mother
must draw out her menses blood
preserved in her body these long years
help me want to talk dream talk
as she scatters red drops on my hair
muttering words from her grandmother's
unwritten diary

Daughters of Artemis

Daughter
in this city
this jumble of ghetto blasters
and glass-splattered sidewalks
panhandlers and condo owners
punkers and Hari Krishna chanters
you cruise your favorite streets
Olive Way, Denny, Broadway
as if you were Jane
lording over your own jungle
walking barefoot
yapping with mohawk owners
sharing cigarettes with scooter friends
dancing in the dark hours
to sounds blaring from a neighborhood deli
and looking at your mother
as if viewing a dinosaur

Well, little girl
I, too
get a fever in my bones
know a boldness
no matador could surpass
my nostrils flare often
(have you noticed?)
smell hot mango sun
I hear rhythms for swaying hips
know I could swim in midnight hours
and devour chocolate sundaes
with sounds that would embarrass you

Let me tell you a secret, young one
I keep a mirror for both of us
silver and gold
studded with rubies
it's sitting on my dresser
ready when you are
waiting for when you hold it to your face
when you hold it to mine
daughter of Artemis

Cactus Prayer

for Larry

We explore an Arizona desert park
chanting cactus plants

teddybear, staghorn cholla

and the redwood of this land
saguaro

we learn their ways
how they get water
what birds live on their fruit and meat
pancake pear, cream cactus

we name, rename
we want a part of this land in us
immerse our human cells in its life
fishhook barrel, desert christmas

we hike all the trails listed
in 102 degree heat
naming, renaming
incantatory
pincushion, prickly pear, hedgehog

yet how can this litany survive
when our rain drenched city greets us?
how do we continue this memory
in 50 degree weather
where mushrooms replace cacti
and the Douglas fir
clouds our memory of the saguaro?

but we are intent
beyond reasoning
we go to another park
with a quart of water
two guide books
and towels to soak up sweat
from our drenched bodies

and we keep repeating
prickly pear
cholla
saguaro

The Demoiselle Remembered

Her folly was sweet as if
all crooked roads led to dance

and zippers caught midway up
while she walked by

Unique like xenon in air
they couldn't keep from following her

each bearing lit frankincense
and bouquets of scarlet roses

My Self Through the Self of My Blood

Someone
whose name has fled my childhood landscape
once told me
my love for rain and thick damp air
are signs of grey dreams, and
I should never mention my desire to
lick up water beads
formed on moss and bark

and a particular voice
(who can say which one,
or how many years back
its sound prickled my skin)
warned me about my wanderings
my seeking people and language not mine
this path
would spew out exotic promises
drive me mad with visions

and it seems a collection of voices
flooding the air around my crib
translated symptoms from a sickness in my head
convinced me later how angry dances
in my weekly nightmares
should be lodged in a secret closet
stored with others whose owners wore masks

and self-proclaimed sages
those who reigned in rigid classrooms
told me I would not survive this world
watching bees gather nectar from clover
meditating on sunsets

even when I started writing poems
new voices groaned over my verse
explained to me the death of rhyme
declared my lines obscure nonsense
and I
with no licensed degree
nor approved modern muse
to guide my pen

So I looked at my self
through the self of my blood
translated sermons from aging parents
decoded words in grandparent diaries
studied books found from dream symbols
until one morning
waking up early
I whispered a new word

Ireland,
where landscapes feast on rain,
and travelers
lured by bog and crag
join farmer and artist
as they stare at sunrise or bee,
where Celtic tales sing of whole clans
seeking other geographies and peoples,
where verse reigns in home and pub
recited as limericks, or in iambic form

where the Sapphos of that country
accept praise for their obscure metaphors
their stanzas shrouded in mystery

and that sickness, called schizophrenia
(the Irish treat it more tenderly)
follows its children to America
challenging future generations

So I studied my mirror
slowly smiling at its reflection
and blessed every one of those voices,
and with that country dancing in my bones
I began writing my next poem

Painting the School White

The parents scream NOT
MY CHILD and in rage or
terror deliver their offspring
to a white painted school
where square classrooms direct
their gait and monitored playfields
bless the children with
straight white teeth

so raw in blood the psychic games
learned, these parents and
their uncles and aunts and
the families' friends
grow blood and terror in
their own homes
as uncle sticks finger
through Suzie's lace panties
and Johnny, age five,
is raped Christmas eve

the parents, trained by
their parents, try sucking
in love to fill up
their bottomless hearts

empty of honey and soft teddy bears,
they run after their children
to beat them behind a proper report card
all the while crying, not knowing how
to swing on a sunny day or calm
their shaking hands
which still continue painting
the school white

Kentucky Wonders

for Jessia Carlson

Height thirsty vines and leaves
spanning two stories' growth
(I touch them from my bedroom window
or from the back door ten feet below)
travel forever upward, creating
meaty, spartan 12 inch long beans

In bunches behind Kelly green leaves
or dangling alone naked and brave
my beans keep coming, keep producing
more Wonders

and not because I compost
or purchase seeds from Burpee
These champions I know keep appearing
because I *will* my beans grow
Mornings before work or
on noon breaks, sitting three feet
from first level vines
Grow I say
you beautiful
crispy, vitamin-packed rawness of
fierce earth
And they grow
sucking up sun, vine and bean
rising beyond second floor, and with
no strings nailed that high
weaving back down and across
sister brother arms

and this fine fast living
pleasing them nicely
until grey dampness of November
and no sun

and how the neighbors talk
with almost lustful sounds about
my beans, helped by fresh memories
of bean gift bags, appearing
on back porches

And Jessia, my 87 year old Irish friend
who yesterday cooked
(for a second time this week!)
her ham chunks and onions and fat slabs
with my green
sunbaked
rainfed
mineral gifted
star legumed
beans

and one mouthful
sending me
oh so much higher
than Jack's climb

This Holy

In the blackness of November nights
I ask if she can be holy.
No, comes the answer, if holy means
cold and death white skin and a body
filled with bloodless air.

But then, I persist, in what way
is she like the others? And then
like sand trickling through my fingers
the words spill out. She is the breath
of Jesus, the mother of Buddha,
rising at dawn like Hercules, pounding
down into earth the sin of old blood.
She is a tall cedar's god, the focusing
of a rose's worship. She swoons
when seeing her own reflection, a mix
of black night and sun, a form
she repeatedly dies for.

Yet I must know this,
for in the silence of morning dreams
I have seen her breathe into newborn mouths,
dance on the skin
of old women, and others say
she brings raw flowers into words,
telling the word owners to push these flowers
through their dead barked bodies.

But now fear grabs hold my guts
and to keep the skeptics from
cutting out my tongue, I practice mumbling
I have never seen her,
nod my head and try sleepwalking again, but
carved cliffs on a sea's lip

call me liar, as does the volcano's lava,
the beetle's eyes, the saguaro's fruit

and I see the ancient grandmothers still alive,
their skin, their cells forever packed
with Her, continue taking this holy
to all our children, even as we birth them
at the crownings, screaming pain and power.

Remembering a Young Girl at the Public Pool

"The only known characteristic found in all Down's syndrome
*children is their great capacity for unconditional love." ***

Japanese cherry petals, rose snow
on April earth, kiss my rain-soaked shoes,
seduce me into singing praises
for all kin of this color,
like scarlet or melon
or wine or camellia

or salmon
like the salmon shade
I once saw in a swim suit.
The young girl who wore this suit
(she was at my local pool),
I see now in these petals
her skin a pink glow, flushed,

like that night when she paddled
from end to end
with Canon in D riding
her squeals of delight.

And I, like one yellow crocus
partly covered
by these blossoms,

peeked out at her from my pool lane
that evening, and later,
embarrassed upon opening her unlocked stall,
still watched her through my mirror
while combing my hair, smiled as she
giggled at two deaf attendants

* *from M. J. Kenney, former aide to special*
  population children, in conversation.

34

who happily scolded her for playing
with toilet paper.

But what silence then permeated that shower
room,
as loud as any high school gym,
where hands started moving to language
I could neither hear nor understand?

"Other abled," already a hackneyed phrase,
keeps floating through my mind,
like the cherry blossoms now falling quietly
from their branches. They say some animals
(is it whales or dolphins?)
talk only to these children.
Maybe I read it in a book.
Maybe I dreamed it.
Would she and the tree
talk about her suit falling off
in the bathroom, about the tree's petals
leaving its branches?

On that same evening, after
she had dressed,
this girl joined other children in the lobby,
all waiting for a van
that drove them somewhere,
other than to the homes
of their births,
where parents will not look into eyes
that give and ask
only for love.

And some of these young ones could sign
with the grace of prima ballerinas,
and their dance softened the concrete walls
and the faces other swimmers wore,
those lucky enough not to have rushed off from
or closed their eyes to
these words
or their owners.

What do they dream?
What lullabies do they crave
as they rest their hands and hearts
for the next day's conversation?
I want to know this

and struggled to get answers right then
to cover my own nakedness
as I sat there fully clothed in that lobby,
and tried to pretend I didn't notice
that I was on the outside,
not even understanding
the jokes that flew

like the hummingbirds
now filling the air
embracing the Japanese cherries.

But when I left the pool,
I waltzed lightheaded
to my yellow-painted car,
held these children's dances
in my own body

skipping lightly
this rainy afternoon,

and as my body learns
their new movements and rhythms
my heart once again sings
wine and scarlet
camellia and melon

and the salmon color
of a swim suit
and one young girl
who filled it.

A Poet's Round

for Barbara Wilson

Oh lines of poetry
big and round
jazz up my words
muscle my sounds

Take me to faerie mounds
under my bed
drive me to drink
in the spider's web

Lines of poetry
cast your round spell
lick up the heavens
living by your well

Comb my heart
shake up my bones
call in five horses
to pull home my poems

Lines of poetry
explode like a rose
make me a rag doll
in your fire's soul

This Winter Rain

heavy and useless like gold
stored in a pope's vault, decides
to slip into the landscape
of my dreams, form ash grey clouds
in my mirror, send its damp breath
into every room of my home

until I no longer remember
how an August sun warms my bones
nor am I able to recall the fragrance
of purple heather, its scent
greeting my aching body
at mountain pass

The sweet cherry tree in my backyard
source of snow-colored blossoms
of red burgundy fruit, as if
involved with the rain's plot
bleeds colorless sap for days, long
before its appointed time at solstice

and even my friend, dead
these four years, decides she wants
my attention Now, but gives
no reasons for her invading
my journal writing, for wringing out
quarts of my tears, for leaving
me empty once again
and still she smiles coyly when I demand
explanations of her portrait

Occasionally I get to an ocean beach,
and the salt foam licking up
my foot prints or the gulls
screeching and bickering, create
an unexplained calmness in my heart,
but those times are as frequent
as the flash of emerald I once saw
from a wood duck's dive

But sometimes I'll shock myself
come upon an amulet I've saved
like today, when sitting at my altar
complaining to Bridget about what
she calls the Irish mist
I saw a dead bee behind her statue
propped against a scallop shell, beady
eyes staring through me

I ran my fingers over its gold fuzz
traced with my pencil designs
I found on its bronzed wings, and
the taste of honey crept
into my mouth and I could smell
pink clover fields, hear buzzing
from its kin on a July day

Tomorrow that rain might still be here
but I've got work waiting for me
like researching the life habits of bees
I want to know how they get honey
or locate flowers miles
from their hive, even when
grey clouds hide the sun
day after unending dark day

I'm in a Stuck Zone

my aura blurred
my visions constipated
Old goals boil dry
in wish pans, love letters
written to nature
crumble in cat's litter box

So what else is new?
Wind fingering my neighbor's birch
asks, and yes, my diploma holds
a conditional degree, letters
lead to nowhere when I put them
in resumes

and too, earth herself
makes no promises, she's
not even immortal, could die
like any star
or planet

but whatever I grasp for
can not be ordered
through a monk's chant, or wished
away in sexual embraces, or
for that matter, gathered
from vigils at Irish wells

I keep howling, though,
for my time grows damnably short
and my dreams won't make
metaphors forever, their pictures
growing dim, as days
march over one another

Ruby

for Renee and Jack

She arrives in a January rainstorm.
And though ruby is Cancer's gem, not
Capricorn's stone, we all forget this fact
as Ruby gurgles and suckles, her corn silk hair
touching her mother's breasts.
And as Ruby smiles, both parents
bloom like wild daisies,
and one Douglas seedling waiting
miles away in cold damp soil
now decides to sprout,
braving residency
on this fragile planet
because (we know!)
Ruby's here.

Erin's Story

The story goes we had it sweet,
beginning as friends, and later
making tides in our bed.
And surely you remember cider
and the taste of donut crumbs
in our teeth. And the cows
(smell of winter barn, of
new cut hay), kicked buckets
of their own sweet milk
over our dreams
more than once.

But how we ever stayed together,
picking out common pieces
of words from two split languages,
hoping against green hope
you would settle the bet
of your unemployed friends.
A bucket of sweet milk
goes far from tongue
to house and round its
kitchen, like a jig
gone mad.

So today you follow a bourn,
find sandprints near campaniles,
their source becoming
your obsession,
while I wait a day or two,
locked in your night's sweat,
our bed to tell my secrets to,
and the sun
blazing the river's skin
as you pass by.

Journal Entry, 17 December '91

My daughter coos in my dreams,
happy at last with her curly
4th grade permanent, her blue eyes
filling my heart's reservoir.

But can she dance in day light?
A woman almost twenty-one, scaling
her nightmares and her father's
unknowing sarcasm.

I write and draw her well,
shaking my pen at smacking monsters
who from the edges of my journal
still hiss and boo my name
called Mother.

Rescue

Told to love in spring
by steamy voices soaking my dreams
I ransomed my best horse for
daylilies, cardinals, and oh yes,
morels pushing through
my borrowed woods.

But really, let's just say
Bridgit wanted help. Some tiny aid
for bringing her troops home.
So many lost ones she lamented
one solstice. By the second of February
she was determined to raise
fire in their hearts.

So, I galloped like any new colt
(though my age defied this description)
and swooped over the dying Celts, crying
Come and jig and reel in true sun!

Of course most laughed, or worse,
ran into their homes, called
state troopers, county sheriffs.
Said a nut's up there in some rented
flying machine
screaming obscenities across
our land.

They couldn't tell, poor souls,
the difference between the dance
and the death march. But like a true
and sincere scalawag, I scooped up
a couple anyway. And
by spring equinox WE knew
our destinies, at least
from that night's splendid tunes,
music branding our hearts for life.

And Bridgit, our lovely
flaming wild one?
She gave us a show we'll
talk about for years.

January's Lesson from Texas

for Charles Dews and David Everett

The giant live oak cradles all below
its old bent arms, still sprouting glazed green
      leaves,
a marvel visiting Yankees can't allow.
Heightened conversations spew out beliefs
stating those garlanded in deciduous dress
must join their winter family portraits nude
or minimally, drop title and select
a name revealing evergreen ties. Some proof
some cone, or needles, visible near their trunks.
Texans don't bother with wasted dead end talk,
sipping iced tea on winter days. While
      chipmunks
(or are those squirrels?) eat acorns they had
      stocked
in autumn when these oaks, these evergreen trees
dropped food, but kept their foliage for our
      soul's feast.

Love Me

for Hattie Gossett

So sure of my word power
I whisper Love Me.
And squirrels bring acorns
to my window. And sun
gleams full right after
I leave work.

I say Love Me Again
and money grows in my purse,
two songs I die for
weep through my radio.

And I face northwest
and for the third time sing
Love Me.
But no voice meets mine.
Mailbox sits empty like a tomb
these last few weeks.

But two out of three!
(A great percentage
in love categories.)
I call myself silly when
I still crawl to bed,
sweat in my fat, sticky,
hating my heart for
its knowing.

SO WHISPER AGAIN
I shout to
no one
except memory curled up
next to my ribs,
pushing me on, saying,
Go For It Girl
And I grin...
loving myself.

Afternoon at Shoal Creek in Austin, Texas

A live oak tree, its knotted limbs,
those long rivers of lined curves,
absorb most all my seeing. And I struggle
to describe this god, inch by
black bark inch.

And my sighting the ball moss, settled
between outer branches, must
explain my inner urgency, in recording
this old giant's existence.

February's last Sunday with bicyclists,
joggers, dog walkers, jugglers,
flooding this Texas park. And the creek
still clear, full, and flowing.

But the oak suddenly spins me into memory:
of farmhouse, of walnut trees, of their limbs
so like this oak's. Four of them
congregated in the back yard.

No! I must forget this farm.
I've plowed that landscape incessantly,
mining for gold or broken bones.
I've cried through six therapists
enduring two collapses.

Yet I can not forget
my cantankerous black Morgan,
the mayflowers and lilacs, baled
alfalfa in our barn's loft, or winter's
rugged waves of snow, or the moon
full on sweet-scented apple blossoms
at midnight
in May.

And those walnut trees.
Harvesting their sweet meat
by the basement's coal bin
on frozen December nights.

The live oak stands solid in its dying,
graceful bony branches, holding
grey green leaves — and the ball moss.
And its body, and the walnuts',
and I guess mine,
breathe for the growing and dying,
like a snake before its last shedding,
like a rock in a volcano's pit.

After Her Ascent

for L. Lennon

Sit out the shadows of my day
and watch moon slowly unearth my new bones.
Here you'll understand cedar's secrets
and know cougar's language after
morning's first heat. And wind's
smooth voice will bring you rest
after these visions.

And too, follow me if fires
threaten to melt my bones, or
if river's swollen belly
hungers for my flesh.

These leaps you take won't bruise
your soul. But it is best to drop
purple hyacinths as you approach, gifts
for hard working snakes and spiders,
who accompany all my days, tasting
air for false messages,
soured hopes.

And be raw for my nights.
Sweetness alone bores even
the strongest. And anyway, my bed
was sewn for the brave ones, those
jumping into a fire's pit
where the phoenix sleeps
after her ascent.

Phone Call

My love for years
embraced the seas
of your heart

but today I swim away

your temple is
growing walls

and I crumble
trying to scale them

Free Woman Poem #1

for Patricia Greene

For my first season in my 49th year
I took a split maple limb and
carved out eight perfect dolls.
And immediately messages
grew in their eyes.
Alarmed by such unplanned events
I buried two of these wooden wonders
right next to my zinnia patch.

From this act
spilling into my dreams that night
I got scared, started cramming chocolate
down the mouths of those left. I couldn't stop
even then, for rain came in buckets
drawing out earthworms from their burrows,
eventually exhuming those two buried dolls.
I gave up completely my sense of justice
and took all eight dolls
to my x lover's house.

How easily I now sleep. I play
my piano until I swoon, the notes
bathing my ears, giving me true reasons
for sobbing.

My dolls, I hear, have been sacked.
But he, my dancer these ten years past,
continues looking for others,
in restaurants,
at movies,
even in his work place,
taking what he finds to bed.

Meanwhile, the zinnia patch
swells with new stalks, new
crispy blossoms.

Taraxacum Officinale

Fresh dandelions
too breathless
for tiny description
push yellow into
landscape.

Lions, now rooted in ground,
roar their sun splashes
at blind motorists.

Hey, see dandelions if
you dare,
between memorizing your latest
sales pitch and planning
your evening meal.

But dandelions are weeds.
We poison these lawn aggressors, grab
any knife, cut out their mustardy assertiveness
at its roots, before they invade
our green space,
our neatly squared off
piece of propertied dirt.

So, few see the dandelions' spring
salad greens, their wine offerings,
the yellow harvest of buttery moons
sprinkled in fields by road ditches.

But dandelions bring forth
and grow old, wispy white seeds
passing onto the land, bearing
new dances for next spring.

And, sometimes, we see them
between moments,
when at country stop signs,
grumbling as we wait.

Lullaby

for Esther "Little Dove" John

1
Sweet pea morning
daughter out of time,
this song composes
your one life time.
And sweet pea morning
daughter out of time,
the cats of the world
can purr your story's line.

> you give us deep pockets
> of spices to wear
> your teeth smile diamonds
> from an organ grinder's tale.

> you whistle to parrots
> such crimson notes
> their feathers respond
> their voices coax.

2
Sweet pea morning
daughter out of time,
is crow the courier
for the languages you find?

> you make potato pie
> you cook Irish stew
> and we clutch our grandma's quilts
> racing after you.

if you want lilacs
spilling into air
if you want perfume
gathered from plum tears,
creatures from Australia
from the Serengeti Plains
offer you help
through the dreaming of their names.

3
Sweet pea morning
daughter out of time,
can't you see
you're our favorite lullaby?

and we won't let you starve
on this grain-filled land again
you'll find no bruises, no violence
forming in our hands.

you'll grow to save the planet
your feet like salve for earth
your skin, colors from each rainbow band
quenching our people's thirst.

4
Sweet pea morning
daughter out of time
Sweet pea morning
our sunrise 'til we die.

Moon Peep

Why not see the moon naked?
And learn about raw messages,
torn dreams? I lick
moon's memory nightly,
to taste the boundaries of
its circled heavens.

And look, moon brings muscled light,
gold for tide's devotion, for
our menstrual direction.

Sure, moon gapes at everything:
lovers making it in car seats,
adult siblings fighting, that
one employee forging checks.
And it's an observer and plunger
combined, screaming yellow jets,
like bright fountains painting
our lives.

Admit it. Each month whether
we just look, or live its
full flush of I am
Moon makes us all lunatics,
all followers of
night's yellow eye.

Children Make

Children make nonsense verse and rhyme,
the words bringing giggles and smiles.

> Clip clap I saw a cat
> riding my donkey to school
> it clawed the brat
> and threw up fast
> donkey now has the flu

Where's the difference? I, an adult,
wrote those words.
"My clipety, clapety, jelopety old lapety"
sends doctors to their clip boards.
Warning! Warning! Warning!
Woman singing nonsense verse. Get
medicine fast. She could start a riot.

I look out at the latest rainfall.
Lightning bolts jog us awake.
So clear, the rhododendron's pink flower.
And what is the clear note sung?
"One or another we laugh in each other."
There, I did it again.

So kids have the fun of nonsense fever.
And while ghosts dance them through sleep,
fountains green with moss, with
bird manure long dissolved,
leave fertile places for
worm's last laugh.

Worm, burn, I'll get it soon
riding my words like horses
gallop, you verb
lasso all curds
and I'll eat adjectives in courses

Oh well, when a language
closes its door to nonsense,
we'll all go to bed, for good,
until — oops, it's coming again!

Frail snail, you snore like hell
bringing frogs to your dance
but I'm painted green
the cricket screams
I'll map your tales in trance

Turnip Memory

Once, when I was tired, and
seeing danger run scared, I
found turnips, waist high.
They set one on another, determined,
firm, bucking the air with their
stern scent. I was afraid
if you want to know the truth.
This too familiar setting caught me
off guard, dissecting my defenses, planting
miniature nightmares in my vision, as if
they knew I kept several in storage.

How such vegetables made poor reputations
astounds me today, and did even then
in my seven-year wisdom.
But I had goals,
a direction to flee. And roses,
crimson and buttercup yellow, beguiled
me with their luscious scent and silk
touch, all abounding in any country yard.

I would have debated staying, if only
the turnips could change their names,
be called tasha bells or maybe trailing spirit.
But that name *turnip* hurt my ears,
sounding like a rock or a dried up cashew.

My grandmother never raised these root vegetables,
growing instead more inviting ones,
guarded by years of soft mushy touches
from her husband, not for
her body, but for young tender children,
their legs and chests, their bottoms.

My grandmother's favorites (bush green beans,
beef steak tomatoes, early asparagus)
she grew to build up her own body,
from a bird-size 75 pounder to a
gargantuan one,
brave and fierce like her father's.

Today I make apologies to the turnips, as I crawl
again over their memories, and wonder about
my tears, soaking my blouse from just
one moments's pause on a turnip field,
only four feet by four, where food
lies waiting, for any eager or curious eater.

Pillow Sonnet

I never can recall my lover's thoughts
that make me bitter when I go back home,
leaving scars inside my head uncaught ·
against my pillow, trying to heal alone.
No one wants to die without rose scent
drifting through a bed where love was bare.
I warn all friends I care for to invent
a dream, of their last breath with no bad scorn.
I ask my sugar maples for a kiss
of sweet sap juice each June when I dream home.
A picture for all lovers seeking clues
and ways to stop these final calls alone.
So I don't hide when eagles crave my flesh
they spot inside my bed's sweet undulant dish.

On the Morning of Mother's Funeral

Mother said once that ages have their own definitions;
and an ancient woman, like herself, until last Sunday,
plays the cards with finesse, building bone
on vitamins, on good beds, on right jogging.
And when anyone wants to make a full step, our
collective physicalities have a way of shooting
for the best planet, of taking our galaxy
by the horns so to speak, and, ultimately, making
our beds with the greatest of planning, as we
walk our alfalfa and wheat days.

Mother said also, and I think this was recent,
"I can accept almost anything coming my way," meaning
any semi or a daffodil pointed in her direction
will equally receive attention, and a slow study
from her mind; that is until this week, when her lungs
and heart stopped their labors, and she had to release
her ways, pass them on to her blooded daughters,
hope we safekeep this talent until our own
time of releasing.

And Mother said (I think more than once), "I try
to accept everyone as they are." This pronouncement
held the greatest challenge, when she herself
would berate her contained body and bones, think
her cum laude status, attached to her college degree,
earned at age 55, was only okay. And she tested
us too, when each of us, her children, the daughters of
this accepting woman, crawled through tunnels,
grotesque creatures and ghoulish language
hitting us at our every move; and those tunnels partly,
and I say only partly, created by this woman.

But Mother made no issue with the state of our being.
She gave us each a bag of presents at our birth
to carry to our own play worlds, while she performed
her Brahms, fed us the best chicken and dumplings
east of the Mississippi,
and praised our mirrors' reflections
and the possibilities of a life
that would always find pomegranates and sunrises.

And if December

And if December

  pulls us through, we'll

    beat the frozen lakes naked

      humming in the night's blackness

        while invisible bugles sound

          yet another birthday

            hopeful

              that life dances

                free

                  and smiling.

New Year's Promise

A pretty woman goes down the street
delivering oranges and melon treats.

You know she arms herself for show, and
perhaps brings dancers to praise her glow.

She dies, though, earnestly every night
afraid fierce dragons have stole her sight;

mining the urban maw for gold
makes her prime target, cellular mold.

I know she's going to charge the sun
for prices she finds mixed with her blood.

And the pretty woman drags home her treats
scoured for, begged for, at every drug meet.

She pins her hopes on her altar space
oh argumentative place of grace.

Bound in her black tights, topping her breasts,
her nipples the crowned statues bearing feasts.

Oh pretty woman, ah daughter true,
your grandmothers have no title on you.

A female born in a paisley tent, an orphan
before tasting your mother's scent.

You play the dice with abandoned souls
who crave their kin in your pupils' glow.

Your beauty, I must tell you, still dissolves
the dread we have of dumping grounds,

those vacant eyes that wander around
a city's holes, its underground.

But bravery bruises your rugged bones
as you make your next bed far from our homes,

homes with enough room for eight of you,
enough food and ample heat for a field of you.

I heard a promise in my dreams last night.
(I woke to feel its words flaming sight.)

You will survive, your life will endure
in poetry and stories I shape next year.

And centuries from this day we'll recite
your battles, your journeys, your sacred rites.

A pretty woman born for the moon
to shine back her life on each quarter's turn.

Bone Story

Once I punished my creativity by
cracking rocks on my dreams, then I
shackled my intelligence building iron
bars around my vocal cords, and soon after
I buried my pulchritude in a body
armed with white lace and a padded smile.
Until, on a brilliant sun fused day,
I stopped, made a decision not to die,
and dove into a jade green lake,
after discarding my survival tools
on a sand dune abutting this emerald womb.
I floated naked, my breasts
pointing toward the sky until it saw me,
the red-tailed hawk. Looking for its day's grub,
this broad-winged buteo took to picking
at my stomach, found new food, carrying
several meals back to its nest. And so my bones
drifted into the water's heart. And so my flesh
found home in the hawk's belly.

Maurine's Last Villanelle

My mother's soul swims down a river of blood
gathering strength each stage it soars on banks.
She lives to bring me home another life.

My mother wills me recipes and vitamins
trying to close this gap of love and fear.
Her photographs forbear her heart's last stop.

I gather roses for her grave each day
yellow blossoms on stone that rise toward the sky.
She lives to bring me home another life.

She takes my dreams some mornings like a storm
rushing in to bring me one lesson more.
Her photographs forbear her heart's last stop.

My body remembers gigues her cello played
and intermezzos her piano still knows well.
She lives to bring me home another life.

I'm married to a language poetry feeds
but sometimes its bony words bleed me dry.
She lives to bring me home another life.
Her photographs forbear her heart's last stop.

Kira's Tanka

Fragrant pea blossom,
why do your scent and color
wake me at sunrise?
Daughter's breath sweet after birth.
Her small body light rose tones.

Paradise

The daughter blooms pink, and a voice
crawls the breast of a mountain, and
her skin makes waves with April's innocent grass,
and the mother sees a new baby, sees the
butterfly with wet wings seeking
the sun's heat, and

the daughter tries planting a tree,
tries growing a willow for its
long draped arms, its soft tender leaves,
but the mother finds knives in the alleys,
sees sleek young women bearing bruises
and old report cards, and

snakes surround an apple orchard,
tongue the air for slick walking carnivores who
feed on sleek young women, foul
the landscape in
their slick silver jackets, and

meanwhile,
the daughter, moves toward the sun, moves
toward the caged lion pacing its boundaries,
and the daughter cuts the bars with her
sea blue eyes, her tight intentions,
and the lion, imprisoned, starved for
Sahara skies, alive only in lion dreams,
leaps for its first kill, the daughter, and

the daughter,
now embraced,
finds her warmth and fury home,
finds power in the flanks of the lion,
finds a form in the cells of this new god,
as together
they go seek paradise.

This Language, This Missal

"...shackling, unshackling the breasts"
from "That Year" by Irish poet Medbh McGuckian

Would anyone kiss thunder? Air responding
with more cracks, yellow jagged lightning
pieces? My mother claimed pure thoughts,
only to escape her husband's hands,
not understanding, either of them, the strength
of coupled passion if done without
shackling each other's bed, each other's nights.

Following pieces, old blood clots, through
flowered sheets, I graze on question marks,
unstated wants, see whole conversations
bleed through box springs, lost forever
between a kiss and a climax.

And I carry this language, this missal,
this dictionary preserved like old photographs
and clothing, stored in our attic, my sisters'
and mine, as they age over the days, bringing
memory to those bald words, uncovering their
resting places.

But now my mother rests too, in some
place called after death, or heaven;
or (I like to think) in a beginning
hillside, where daffodils proliferate
its surface, hungry to eat the black soil,
soak under one April sun.

Thalassa

1

the sea, blasting a fog horn, cracking the air
loosens my throat. (I am at least opened
by its sirenic damp wind.)
my soul leaks its identity, like burning coal,
showing its design, its filtered red blood heat
melting uncautiously into the water's briny arms.

2

curling itself
into back biting waves, this ocean
holds its benthic ground, its
own power roaring from other lands.

this buttress of cold and salt
treats its onlookers
to a bulging field of trembling glitter,
with sun pouring its skin on ocean's surface
while moon, still white yellow slit, drips
onto the water's face, brings me to
the we of others, cracks my bone memories
pouring them into this pelagic dance.

and this ocean, a full
mesmerized ionized
notion of thickness
puts the gull at risk
the brown pelican in hold.
and killdeers run to their nests.

3

I sit alone on this wet land
with millions of others
on this salty clothed beach
of drowned dreams, of cardinal red illusions,
of heartbeats looking for answers
in the clipped rhythms they sometimes beat out.

and the ocean breaks my solid winter heart,
breaks the road I had made
in orders written on my cells taken
from their outer shells, though
marked highway, marked dead.

insistent, and pounding on, this world tub
of power water
this galactic birth sack
unbinds the crippled words,
rips up all the I's and solitudes of
other, everywhere
and carries us to a place marked
Honey, marked Limb Dancing Limb, marked
Tales To Breathe By.

Tree of Power

Sometimes
I say to a tree
Don't be so naked and raw
in your beauty, or I may lose it
and dance forever on your limbs
or sit next to you naked myself
in a very un-buddhalike

p

o

s

e

howling my stories to anyone wandering by...

Photo: Anna Johnson

PAT ANDRUS, born and raised on a farm in Michigan, and formed by Irish-Catholic and German-Scotch clan lines, moved to the Northwest in 1968 where she now resides with her husband Larry and daughter Kira. Her poems appear in local and national publications. In 1987 a letterpress collection of her verse *Daughter* was published by Olivewood, in Seattle. With Texas poet and writer Charles Dews and Northwest musician Mariana Van Blair, Andrus produced *Beágan: The New Branch,* a recording of Celtic American poetry and Irish music, through Toora Loora Loora Press / Spoken Arts in 1991. An adjunct faculty member for Bellevue Community College's English Department, Andrus has served as faculty for the Sitka Fine Arts Camp and as Artist In Residence for the State of Washington (1991-1993). In addition to writing and teaching, Andrus studies contemporary dance and movement theater with choreographers Debra Hay, Jeff Bickford, and Tom Truss.